A Pumpkin Pie Worth Leaving Tennessee For
Essays on the Sustainable Life from Fast, Cheap, and Good

Jennifer Patterson Lorenzetti

Copyright © 2019 Jennifer Patterson Lorenzetti
All rights reserved.
Published by Hilltop Communications
www.hilltopcommunications.net

ISBN-13: 978-1-7325734-1-3

DEDICATION

As always, this is for my family:

My parents, Michael and Janice Patterson
My husband, Daniel Lorenzetti

And to our pup, Shinnosuke, who thinks my pumpkin pie is well worth making a trip anywhere.

Contents

Chapter 1: Life Hacks 7

Chapter 2: Sustainable Habits 31

Chapter 3: Finances 57

Chapter 4: News and Issues 67

Chapter 5: Humor 83

Chapter One: Life Hacks

Jennifer Patterson Lorenzetti

A Pumpkin Pie Worth Leaving Tennessee For

Saving Your Sanity at Christmas

If you celebrate Christmas, the period of time between Thanksgiving and January 2 can rapidly turn from being a time for joyful celebration into a part-time job you didn't really ask for. And, judging by some of the posts I've seen on Facebook from some of my friends, the season is bringing with it its standard array of frayed nerves and mood swings. That's why I want to talk about a kind of sustainability we rarely talk about here -- saving your own sanity.

Christmas is some high-stakes stuff. Religiously, you have the story of a miracle more precious and perfect than any that has ever occurred. On the secular front, you have Currier & Ives, Norman Rockwell, and the entire cartoon and stop-motion animation industries conjuring up pictures of the perfect family holiday. Even if you don't celebrate Christmas at all, you can't avoid the pressure -- it is there in the aisles of your grocery store (who doesn't need some extra tinsel?) and on your car radios and in your newspaper advertising supplements. It is enough to make anyone bonkers.

Add to that the fact that annual holidays really can bring on the melancholy. If we look back, we see Christmases spent with relatives now departed or with innocence and hope that we may no longer have. If we look forward, we might fear what we could lose in the year to come, or what storms we might have to weather before we put up that tree again. (This is a big one for me.) It takes a better yogi than I am to stay perfectly balanced in the present.

So, as my gift to you, let me offer a few tips for how to get through the holiday with a minimum of mental angst and a maximum of joy. Remember, your sanity is a limited resource you must use in a sustainable way too!

Limit the Christmas Music/Specials: Now, if you're one of those people who only gets happier the more carols that play, you'll want to ignore me on this one, but I suggest you limit the number of Christmas TV specials you watch and Christmas songs you hear. The reason? I don't want to be a Scrooge, but these reminders of the season, by their very nature, bring back memories and tug at the heart strings with holiday reminders. If you find yourself thinking of your departed aunt every time you listen to her favorite Christmas song or tearing up whenever you watch the special your kids loved when they were small, do yourself a favor and turn it off. Save your exposure for things that really make you happy.

Stay Off Social Media: While we're limiting our media, this may be a good time to place a rationing system around your use of Facebook and the like. I know it is tempting to spend part of your time off work continually hitting "refresh" on your phone, but you need to limit the number of times you see examples of Christmas perfection posted by your friends. It brings a tear to anyone's eye to see the picture of four generations of women, all gathered in the kitchen with well-starched aprons, happily making cookies. Try to remind yourself that your friend posted that photo not because it is an everyday occurrence in their happy lives, but because they thought, "Dang, I've never seen that kind of thing happen in my life -- better snap a picture and post it to Facebook and prove it actually happened!"

Take Some Shortcuts: We've all read the holiday stories of cooks who make a pie for every holiday guest so everyone will have their favorite, or of those who have time to paint little decorated packages on their fingernails, complete with bows and nametags. (Bonus Tip: Stay off Pinterest!) You don't have to do this. If you hate making pie and you feel you must make one, make ONE. Everyone's just going to have to make do with the flavor you chose. Don't allow yourself to feel pressured into doing everything you think everyone expects just to make a perfect holiday. Which leads me to my next tip...

Remember that Santa Had Elves: Even the mythical Big Guy didn't try to throw a celebration without help. Now is your time to ask people to help you with the tasks you think are essential. Go ahead, ask your mother-in-law to bring dessert; if you ask her to bring that specialty her son or daughter always loved growing up, I'll bet she says "yes." If you feel you must be the sole host or hostess of an event, for heaven's sake wait until the summer barbeque, when you don't have do a million other things besides.

A Pumpkin Pie Worth Leaving Tennessee For

Allow Yourself to Remember: Even if you have the logistics mastered, Christmas can bring some strong emotions, particularly if your family is missing a loved one. Give yourself time to remember, and allow those feelings to be bittersweet. Honor that person in a way that is meaningful to you; hang an ornament that reminds you of them, or make their favorite recipe, and invite this person back into the celebration.

Save Something for You: "Christmas is for children." "Christmas is for other people." Yes, the spirit of these sayings is very true and well-taken. But if you get wrapped up in making a holiday for others, you will miss it yourself. Pick something that you look forward to; one thing for me is Christmas Eve dinner with just my husband. Then, tell everyone that this part of the celebration is important to you, and you really want to see it happen. After all, it is important to give, but it is important to nourish your own soul so you can keep giving in the New Year.

Jennifer Patterson Lorenzetti

One-Off Wednesdays

According to a study by the University of Michigan Institute for Social Research, in 2005 married women with no children did an average of 17 hours of housework each week. Housework here is defined as chores like "washing dishes, laundry, vacuuming floors, and dusting," otherwise described as work "people generally do not enjoy doing." I'd quibble with that; I really love to do those chores; they give me a sense of satisfaction and accomplishment I don't get from anything else.

However, with a full time job (and with other important chores, like gardening, not included in this list because they are considered to be more pleasant by the researchers), it is a struggle to get my 17 hours to do my housework. And, honestly, even though I love the routine stuff, I will admit that it does have a tendency to never be done -- doing laundry today doesn't mean there won't be more laundry tomorrow.

That's why my favorite day is "One-Off Wednesdays." For the rest of the week, I try to follow a schedule of laundry, fluffing and folding, baking, cleaning bathrooms, changing sheets, and running the vacuum, but on Wednesday I get to pick a periodic chore that rarely gets the attention it deserves, and really dive in.

One day, the chore was cleaning the bedroom floor with diluted oil soap. After vacuuming the rug, I got down with a rag and my soap, and I really did a good job of cleaning the hardwood, including the corners, the woodwork, and the furniture legs. My floor looked so shiny, and the bedroom smells amazingly clean!

Other chores for One-Off Wednesday?

- Polish the brass on the fireplace and clean the ashes out into the ash bucket (the ashes will go by cups-full into the compost bucket to reduce odor and eventually be composted into new humus to nourish the garden).
- Clean all the doorknobs.

A Pumpkin Pie Worth Leaving Tennessee For

- Use glass cleaner on everything glass in the house -- mirrors, glass table tops, glass TV screens.
- Beat the throw rugs with my rug beater; in the winter, snow wash them first.
- Dust the chandeliers and the corners where the walls meet the ceilings.

You get the idea. These are the fiddly little things you wish you had time to do more of, and Wednesday is my day to indulge.

Cycles of Sustainability

I have a confession: Along with many other sustainable living experts, authors, and bloggers, I'm guilty of making it sound like sustainable living can be broken down into a lot of little projects, with a huge focus on gardening, food preservation, and vintage-style domestic arts.

This is true, to some degree. But, if you don't take a systemic view of your lifestyle, you may find that you have simply changed your daily activities without making a noticeable improvement in your life.

Remember our fundamental purpose: sustainable living means responsible use of resources. Resources include food, clothing, land, environment, time, money, health, or anything else that you may have a demand for that exceeds the supply.

To that end, I thought it might be useful to share the overall structure of my year, which I divide into three "seasons."

Season One (January-April): Focus on Earning

The winter months are cold and dreary around here, and I am not exactly a cold-weather person. Therefore, I find it helpful to throw the majority of my energy behind projects that maximize my income, since it's too cold outside to do much in the way of gardening.

Major Activities
- Work on as much writing as possible.
- Take on extra teaching assignments. One winter term, I taught eight credit hours of classes in addition to my primary writing biz.
- Add photos and projects to our photography and design web sites.
- Continue to sell and work on restocking my Etsy store.

Minor Activities
- Start garden plants.
- Do non-vegetable canning, like stock from meat bones.

A Pumpkin Pie Worth Leaving Tennessee For

Season Two (May-August): Focus on Saving
This is my favorite season. Nearly every day brings time in the garden, and I have more time to work on various projects. During this season, I focus on projects that will either generate income or save time or money in the coming months.

Major Activities
- Keep the garden in full production.
- Make as many meals as possible from primarily garden products, reducing expenditures for food and improving health.
- Preserve as much food as possible, reducing future food bills, speeding future meal production, and improving health.
- Buy food I don't grow at the farmer's market, with lower in-season prices. Preserve any extra.
- Institute energy saving projects, like drying laundry on the line, using passive solar heat to warm the house or open window to cool when possible, and taking advantage of long days to avoid using lights throughout the house.
- Work on writing projects that will sell year-round, for a passive income stream. Right now, my focus is on my book-length projects.
- Continue to maintain regular writing and photography work.

Minor Activities
- Split wood for fall home heating, when there are many days we can heat exclusively or primarily with our wood stove.
- Continue to stock the Etsy store.
- Catch up on seasonal home projects that weather or time constraints will make impractical later, such as weatherproofing, necessary home improvements, or even just washing and line-drying all the quilts and bedding in the house.
- Conduct "expenditure audit," looking at things like cell phone plans, video streaming service usage, gym memberships, and the like, and cancelling or altering the things that no longer fit our needs.

Season Three (September-December): Focus on Processing

I've been in academia so long that I almost reflexively think the year begins in September. This is the season that many of the projects I've worked on all year pay off and I have time to think about the next cycle.

Major Activities
- Process orders in the Etsy Christmas rush. Crochet like a mad woman to continue to keep existing stock in the store as high as possible by replacing items as they sell.
- Plan meals around canned, frozen, and still-growing garden products and other such preserved food (like chickens purchased "in season" over the summer at harvest time). Attempt to keep grocery bill low by relying on food in stock.
- Pick up teaching load again. Typically, my fall semester load is lighter than my winter/spring one, but that can change according to need.
- Continue to write and photograph.
- Institute heat-saving and -generating measures around the house, like use of the wood stove, venting the dryer inside, using passive solar heat, and getting those freshly sunned quilts out of the closet.

Minor Activities
- Generate ideas for future writing projects. Keep a OneNote file on each so that I can work on them year round as time permits.
- Focus on non-food sustainability projects like rebatching soap.

A Pumpkin Pie Worth Leaving Tennessee For

The Power of Going Outside

Normally, I focus on sustainable use of resources like time, money, food, and fuel; all important things. But here, I'm going to focus on something else that's easy to use up and hard to get back: your sanity. Because I've become at least half convinced that our modern lifestyle is killing us.

Think about what we do every day. Now, I'm lucky, in that part of the year I have the freedom that comes with self-employment and good weather to take a bike ride to the grocery or to see a client, but the majority of us are stuck for several hours in a day sitting in a chair behind a desk staring at a screen. Everything is square and backlit and makes strange beeping noises, particularly when you get email that explains why this deadline has been moved up or that client needs something right away or another person needs something fixed. These things may be our financial lifeblood, and they may even provide a degree of career satisfaction, but, no matter how benign, they take a toll on our health.

One study out of Australia that goes a long way toward quantifying our need for nature in our lives. According to the research, if everyone visited a park for just 30 minutes once a week, there would be "seven percent fewer cases of depression and nine percent fewer cases of high blood pressure." That's pretty specific, but it does point out that we can get a lot of benefit from even a little exposure to nature. It also maybe suggests that if corporations were really serious about employee health, they'd make sure they had some green space and encourage everyone to use it.

Of course, it's difficult sometimes. In the winter, I often think of my father, who used to work in a windowless office. In the winter, he'd go to work in the dark and come home in the dark with only glimpses of the sun. Needless to say, my sun-loving father always had trouble with this arrangement.

The fact is, our bodies -- and that includes our minds -- need the outdoors. We evolved to want the warmth of the sun and the development of vitamin D in our skin. We spent millennia evolving a comfort with irregular, organic shapes and leafy green canopies above our heads. We have a visceral memory of the comfort of salt water, the salinity of which is echoed in every cell in the human body. We love nature because we evolved to be a part of it.

Now, I'm not arguing against progress. Believe me, I like central heat and ready supplies of food and electronic gadgets as much as the next person. But we all have to take time to touch base again with nature. Our minds will thank us for it.

A Pumpkin Pie Worth Leaving Tennessee For

"Sunlight and Vitamin D: Necessary for Public Health" An Academic Review

Writing in the Journal of the American College of Nutrition, a group of authors have published "Sunlight and Vitamin D: Necessary for Public Health[1]." The study is a fascinating one.

Basically, the authors examine the fact that many recommendations from the American Cancer Society, the World Health Organization, and the like, focus on encouraging sun avoidance and sunscreen use during the very hours of the day that our bodies are most primed to make use of the sun:

"Though these recommendations, all focused on reduction of skin cancer, are accompanied by brief acknowledgement of the importance of vitamin D for health, they persist in urging avoidance of the sun at the precise times when vitamin D can be synthesized in the skin—the hours between 10 am and 3 pm—and suggest that all necessary vitamin D can be obtained through food and dietary supplements."

And yet, there are compelling reasons to get your Vitamin D from the sun. Take a look at this introductory paragraph:

"These recommendations are understandable from the viewpoint of preventing the 3.5 million new cases of and 2000 deaths from nonmelanoma skin cancer in the United States each year, but they neglect the fact that we have a long cultural history of appreciation of the sun and use of UV radiation for healing purposes. Moreover, they neglect that we have evolved with physiological adaptations to help protect the skin from the sun when we are mindful of our exposure and do not burn. They neglect the fact that increased sun exposure, based on latitude, has been associated with protection from several different types of cancer, type 1 diabetes, multiple sclerosis, and other

---

[1] Baggerly, C. A., Cuomo, R. E., French, C. B., Garland, C. F., Gorham, E. D., Grant, W. B., ... Wunsch, A. (2015). Sunlight and Vitamin D: Necessary for Public Health. Journal of the American College of Nutrition, 34(4), 359–365. http://doi.org/10.1080/07315724.2015.1039866

diseases. They also neglect the fact that exposure to the sun induces beneficial physiological changes beyond the production of vitamin D. Though adherence to the current sun-protective recommendations would likely result in the reduction of nonmelanoma skin cancer, that reduction would likely be overshadowed by the potential reduction in deaths from other cancers and from cardiovascular disease, which could be achieved by doubling average blood concentrations of 25-hydroxyvitamin D (25(OH)D) to 40 ng/mL through a combination of sun exposure and supplements."

Let's break that down a bit. Basically, we're saying that, in our zeal to protect ourselves from approximately 2000 nonmelanoma skin cancer deaths a year, we are turning our backs (no pun intended) on our cultural and biological adaptations that allow us to appreciate the sun and use it for healing. Additionally, we are increasing our risk of other types of cancer, type 1 diabetes, multiple sclerosis, and other conditions.

For example, look at these benefits:

"When the skin is stimulated with UVA radiation, nitric oxide is released, stimulating vasodilation and lowering of blood pressure. During active exposure to UVA, diastolic blood pressure in one study fell by roughly 5 mmHg and remained lower for 30 minutes after exposure. A reduction of diastolic blood pressure by 5 mmHg decreases risk for stroke by 34% and coronary heart disease by 21%."

"Additionally, human skin produces beta-endorphin in response to UVB exposure; these opioid peptides have the result of increasing a feeling of well-being, boosting the immune system, relieving pain, promoting relaxation, wound healing, and cellular differentiation. Light signals received through the eye regulate production of melatonin and serotonin for circadian rhythm control and also play a role in seasonal affective disorder."

Short form: sunlight contains both UVA and UVB radiation. The UVA radiation can lower blood pressure enough to decrease risk for stroke and coronary heart disease. UVB radiation can improve mood, help with certain depressive conditions, improve the immune system, relieve pain, and help with healing.

Are we sure we want to keep avoiding the sun?

Look, no one is going to tell you to go try to get a sunburn. And if vitamin D supplements make sense to you, go for it. But the sun has been getting a bad rap lately.

And, there are reasons for seeking the sun:

"The full solar spectrum is essential to optimal health and well-being. Humans are physiologically adapted to produce vitamin D in response to sun exposure, specifically UVB radiation; other regions of the spectrum seem to confer benefit as well. Though some vitamin D comes from our diet (and more recently from supplements), we should not ignore the natural capacity that we possess to produce our own. We are of the opinion that moderate sun exposure (less than the time required to burn) to the arms, shoulders, trunk, and legs should be sought rather than avoided."

I agree with the authors. Bottom line, the full spectrum of sunlight seems to confer many health benefits, and our bodies are designed to make vitamin D from this exposure. So go outside wearing a tank top and shorts. Mow the lawn, hang the laundry, take a bike ride. Do so between the hours of 10 am and 3 pm for maximum formation of vitamin D. As long as you don't allow yourself to burn, you will very likely be helping your health far more than you might possibly harm it.

Plan the Work and Work the Plan

As a college instructor, I notice that we spend a lot of time telling young adults to follow their dreams and to find work that they enjoy so much they "never work another day in their lives." I love the sentiment. May we all find pursuits in life that are the most pleasant and rewarding ever.

However, even your favorite job - even the best aspects of your favorite job - will sometimes drag you down. Sometimes, there are days when you are simply unmotivated; sometimes, work hits a rough patch or you simply have to do things you are not in the mood to do.

I'm not immune to these feelings, and it is never easy to struggle through a patch of low motivation, but I do have a system that helps me stay productive during those times. I divide my work into roughly two "moods:"

Dreaming, Planning, and Executing

These are the days when motivation is high. It's not that these days don't involve work; indeed, some of my best productivity comes during my planning and executing days. But these are the days that the clouds part and I can see the big picture, and one thing I'm sure to do is make lists. I make lists of all the things that need to be done to reach my long-term and intermediate goals, and I break everything down into individual tasks, ranging from making copies of documents to outlining new books. Everything goes on a list.

I also execute the difficult stuff that requires a lot of brain work. So, I won't make copies on days of high energy, but I will do a book outline (I must have 5 books in the queue behind the one I'm currently writing), rework a lesson for class, design a new product for my Etsy store, or market for new work. These are also great days to get lots of writing done, and these are the days to make lots of necessary phone calls, because I'm probably feeling gregarious.

Work the Plan

Inevitably, though, I will have a day when work seems

A Pumpkin Pie Worth Leaving Tennessee For

insurmountable, and I just don't have the energy to go forward. The goals seem so impossibly far away, to say nothing of the dreams. Working hard seems an exercise in futility.

That's when I pull out the lists. I tell myself that I don't have to do anything big or far reaching; I just have to cross things off those lists. That's when the photocopying comes in, or the filing. These are the days for research that involves looking up specific facts for an article or sending bunches of emails to people who need information or who I need to get information from. And these are great evenings for simply sitting and churning out crocheted items for sale.

The ultimate point is that these lower motivation days may not be the most fun or the most inspirational, but work keeps moving forward. Tasks keep getting done, and I'm making progress toward the goal, even if it doesn't feel like the goal will ever be reached. Then, the next time I'm well-motivated, I have all of the little tasks done, and I can once again think big because I can once again see the big picture.

Jennifer Patterson Lorenzetti

On the Value of Going Old School

I was researching an article about certain kinds of tech, and I started looking into fitness watches. You know: those strap-on devices that only incidentally tell time; their real purpose is to count your steps, use GPS to track the route you walk or run or bike, and maybe even gather certain biometric data like heart rate. I have to admit they are cool, and there's part of me that wants one.

A couple of days later, I was in a conversation with some college instructors who were admitting to going old school. One, like me, uses a paper planner. Another uses a traditional, paper grade book. For these instructors (and for me), there are certain kinds of information that we find most accessible and easiest to manage by using a pencil and paper.

It got me to thinking about the role that technology plays in our lives. I like to think that I'm not a technical Luddite; the other day, I posted a picture to Facebook of my office, in which I had no fewer than four screens spread across three computing devices open, active, and in use. My favorite device right now is my iPad mini, which has replaced a laptop in a lot of situations for me.

But, for other things, I like to go old school. I like my paper planner; I can't quite get the same grasp on the cycle of my day and my to-do list by flipping back and forth between apps on my phone. My all-time favorite laptop replacement, which I have written about before, was my AlphaSmart; sadly, I can no longer get it to sync with any of my more modern devices, meaning I cannot write on it and extract what I have written. I've been thinking fondly of the days when your cell phone could make and receive calls, maybe do some very clunky texting, and play a game or two, instead of operating as a mobile office, productivity suite, and entertainment center that costs several hundred dollars and which you are terrified of losing or breaking.

Technology is great. If we were to completely eschew technology and took this to extremes, we would not have the wheel, the loom, or the most basic of knives. Technological progression helps us move

A Pumpkin Pie Worth Leaving Tennessee For

forward as a species.

But sometimes, technology leads us instead of us leading technology. What good is a productivity device if you spend all of the time you have saved reworking your work flow and buying new connectors, adapters, and chargers that fit an ever-changing array of devices. For example, I have "solved" the problem of how to work on an airplane and on vacation no fewer than six times over the past 20 years, and every time devices change, I have to rethink my preferred solution.

I don't know the answer, but maybe the next time I go on vacation, I'll take a legal pad and a few pencils. They'll work anywhere, they never lose their charge, and I don't have to worry (much) about them being stolen. And, my writing always was better when it occurred at the pace dictated by my own hand and when I edited it while I typed up the final version.

Jennifer Patterson Lorenzetti

On Using the Good China

I was looking at some advertising from the 1940s and 1950s the other day, when post-war affluence met demographic trends to create the bridal industry that we know today, and I started thinking about how much I love my good china.

It grieves me, on some level, to think that I may be part of the last generation of brides to even want good china. The day after we got engaged, Mr. FC&G and I went to the department store and registered for our china, silverware, and other items. I remember how excited I was to finally - finally - get this lovely, delicate stuff and to have it displayed in my china cabinet. (Buying the china cabinet, which I had done years earlier, should have been my first clue that I was on the end of a demographic trend, because it took trips to many, many stores to find something that would function as such. No one offered a "china cabinet" per se.) Receiving the beautiful boxes of china as wedding gifts thrilled me, and, to this day, I stop and look at my china every time I walk into the dining room.

It made me sad when, a decade or so ago, I started reading reports of how people were no longer buying good china. They were afraid of breakage, they didn't want to wash it by hand, and they wanted the money to spend on something else. More power to them, I suppose. However, I also became aware, through personal experience, that no one knows how to act around good china any more.

I have let myself become shamed out of using the good stuff, because it invariably sparks some sort of contentious moment in which I either be a good hostess and let my guests have what they want, or I stand my ground. Since I am of the school of thought that holds that a good hostess, upon seeing her guest drink from the finger bowl, resolutely takes a swig out of her own, I usually wind up capitulating.

I have had guests hand plates back to me, asking for something not so precious and saying that they can eat off anything - and that's just when I'm using my second-best, "everyday" china that was my "good

A Pumpkin Pie Worth Leaving Tennessee For

stuff" from when I was single. I have nearly bitten my tongue off to refrain from saying that, if they can eat off anything, surely they can figure out how to eat off a plate that I didn't buy in a boxed set in grad school.

I have had visitors charge into my kitchen and plunge their hands into my everyday silverware drawer, unwilling to wait until I retrieve a matched set for their use. "Oh, don't go to any bother; I can get it," they say. But maybe I wanted to offer something nice for their use, and it's not like I don't have a couple of complete, matched sets of dessert forks that I can use to serve people.

I have even had people hand cloth napkins back to me and ask for a paper napkin. On that one, I have no choice but to protest, because I don't own any paper napkins, save for maybe a pack of birthday-themed ones shoved into the back of the pantry. I haven't otherwise purchased paper napkins in over a decade. I've learned to hide the paper towel roll if I have people over for a summer cookout, because they will invariably refuse to pick up a cloth napkin from the buffet and tell me that I shouldn't have to wash the cloth napkins. Really, folks, it's no trouble; I put them in the washer and hang them outside to dry. I'm not exactly washing them on a wash board and then starching and ironing them.

In short, I have let myself succumb to peer pressure to not enjoy and share my finest possessions, even though doing so brings me great joy. I want people to know that they mean a great deal to me, and that they are worth me creating an elegant experience. Am I going to serve picnic food outside on the good china? Probably not. But I derive a lot of pleasure from using the china, the good silverware, and the pretty cloth napkins to enjoy a meal with friends or family. To me, it is my reward for serving my guests.

So, no more of this. From here forward, the good china is coming out of hiding once in a while, if only just for my husband and I. We have long planned that, when we retire, we will get rid of the kitchen table and take only the good dining room table to our new home, and that we will likely use the china as well. I think that should start today. We deserve the joy of using the nicer things, and, if you are invited to our house, I hope you will do so too.

A Pumpkin Pie Worth Leaving Tennessee For

Driving as a Sustainable Skill

I've always hated to drive. Although I occasionally have the opportunity to drive a car that I really enjoy being behind the wheel of, mostly I view it at best as a necessary evil of transportation and at worst as a boring chore punctuated by occasional demonstrations of other drivers' idiocy.

But I can drive, and I daresay I drive well. And I have been driving for as long as I have been legally allowed. Although my memory is hazy on the specifics of 1980s Indiana driver's license law, I do remember that those of us who took a driver's ed class could get our licenses a month past our sixteenth birthday. This is how I wound up at the DMV after a major snow in December, proving that I could drive on slick roads and avoiding idiots who wouldn't adjust their speed for conditions. I still think I was exempted from the parallel parking test in part because I skillfully avoided getting hit by one of these speeding idiots, and in part because there were no parking spots not filled with snow drifts. Nonetheless, I was unwilling to wait so much as an extra week for better testing conditions; proving that I had the skill and could achieve the rite of passage were that important to me.

But lately, I've noticed a change. Young people don't drive. And it isn't just that they don't drive, it's that they can't drive. I know many young -- and not so young -- people who don't have driver's licenses and who depend on others to ferry them around. The fact that AAA can run an advertisement trying to encourage parents to goad their adult children into learning to drive before college starts shows just how much things have changed.

Learning to drive, in this society, is just as important a sustainable living skill as knowing how to grow your own food. And while I don't want to insult those who choose not to drive, I think that not being able to or legally allowed to is an unnecessary sacrifice of potential independence.

This is not to say that I think extensive, unnecessary driving is a good idea. You don't have to drive to do your errands if you can make a bike work for you. Carpooling to school or work is a great idea. Heck, you don't even have to own a car if you don't want to.

But for heaven's sake, and, more importantly, for your own protection, learn how to drive a car and become legally licensed to do so. You never know when you will get caught in a situation when you are the only available driver and you need to be able to drive competently: a small child in your care has to get medical care or you are out with friends that become ill or incapacitated. You also never know when being able to use this tool -- and a car is a tool -- will help you live a more traditionally sustainable or frugal life. City dwellers might borrow a Zip Car occasionally to stock up at a far-flung farmer's market or warehouse club. Those in suburbs and rural areas will find that driving is essential to access many of the resources you need for living, at least occasionally.

If you don't have a driver's license, please: learn to drive and get licensed. What you do after that is your call.

Chapter 2: Sustainable Habits

Jennifer Patterson Lorenzetti

A Pumpkin Pie Worth Leaving Tennessee For

Barriers to Biking

I read a wonderful article on barriers to women biking more, and I was fascinated by the reasons that women don't opt to bike as much as they might. When my part of Ohio braces for the first snowfall of the year, I find myself yearning for a little errand on my bike, knowing that I will be waiting until Spring for that to happen.

The article breaks down the barriers to women biking into five main types:

> Risk
> Time
> Convenience
> Vanity
> Community

I must admit that I have forgone biking for all of these reasons from time to time. And, with the possible exception of vanity, I think they are equally valid for men, too.

For me, one of the top barriers is risk, including comfort issues. I won't bike in the snow or ice. Truthfully, I won't bike with temps in the 50s or lower. I won't bike in the rain. I know there are readers from very bike-centric cities that are laughing at me for this, but I don't always feel safe or comfortable in these conditions. Add onto that the fact that some trips don't feel physically safe to me to do alone. For example, one errand I could run involves a bike path that is very secluded; I will bike it happily with Mr. FC&G, but I won't bike alone.

Second for me is definitely vanity. And, unlike some bikers, I have no belief that I have to be wearing spandex and biking shoes to get on my bike; I bike in A line skirts and chunky heels half of the time. In my finest moments, I have biked in stilettos. Let me tell you, a good stiletto heel is as good as a toe clip for keeping your foot on the pedal. However, there are times that I don't feel like re-doing my hair when I get to my destination, or I just don't care to bike to a meeting or a class and have to commit to a ponytail for the whole day.

Finally, there is community. There is something wonderful about a community that embraces walking and biking as viable types of transportation. One of the things I love about Key West is the bike culture. Everyone goes everywhere on a bike, so there is no question in your mind that you will find a place to chain up your bike or that the motorists will be unaware of the possibility of bikers (so, overlapping with risk). Also, the casual culture and the warm environment means that you will probably be wearing flip flops and comfy skirts and ponytails anyway, just to handle the climate. There is less call to look "professional" on a daily basis (although I do love dressing up for clients, so I would miss it). The culture of your community makes a huge difference.

A Pumpkin Pie Worth Leaving Tennessee For

Why Drought Means You Must Garden

From time to time, parts of the country face a serious drought. Farmers predict low yields on the corn and soy that seem to find their way into every grocery store product, and prices on meat and dairy are expected to go up because factory-farmed cattle (unnaturally) eat mostly the corn that is in short supply.

Frugality blogs and news stories respond with hints about ways to stock up and find deals in the coming months. While these tips are generally very helpful, I'm going to take a different position and say that, in difficult growing times, you MUST plant a garden.

Why do I think you can succeed where large farms cannot?

Your microclimate: Even if you are sitting in the middle of the worst of the heat wave and drought, your own microclimate may lend itself to production of vegetables large farmers can't grow. A shade tree, a porch for your container garden, or just a slightly low spot in your yard can all make a degree or two difference in temperature and can have different water needs.

Your irrigation needs: Factory farmers simply can't irrigate as much as they would need during a drought, and they sometimes are growing crops so closely spaced that their water needs are even greater. You, on the other hand, can surely pull out the watering can or hose to douse your small garden. Space your plants a little farther apart so they have more root space to dig for water.

Transportation: Once farmers harvest their paltry drought-damaged crops, the crops have to be transported multiple times for processing and sale in your area. In case you haven't noticed, fuel prices aren't dropping either, so you will also pay your portion of those increases. Why pay to transport crops out of the drought area to your store if you can just go outside and grab your dinner from your yard?

Flexibility: The large farmers have to grow certain varieties of crops that can grow densely and can withstand the treatment they get, which in many cases mean they grow GMOs and other questionable hybrids instead of heirlooms. A lot of this is driven by economics and scale on which they operate. You, as the small gardener, are not confined in this way. One year, we grew carrots over the winter in a raised bed protected by a cold frame, grew a crop of leeks that matured in winter (again protected by a cold frame), and grew potatoes in a container You can do likewise with your space.

None of this is meant as a diatribe against individual farmers in the large farm system. In many cases, I think these hard-working men and women wanted to hold onto a traditional way of life and have been slowly squeezed by governmental, economic, and corporate pressures into farming highly-modified varieties of crops in monoculture -- ironically, exactly the recipe for failure in any kind of temporary shift in the weather. It will take a culture change to fix those problems.

In the meantime, those of us with small gardens can relieve some of the demand and help our own budgets by growing locally. Now more than ever, you really need to garden.

A Pumpkin Pie Worth Leaving Tennessee For

Join Me for National Hanging Out Day

Have you heard about National Hanging Out Day? If you are like most of my readers and are embracing the sustainable living lifestyle, you probably call this another name, like "Wash Day." For the uninformed, this is the annual "holiday" celebrating the time-honored tradition of hanging one's wash outside to dry.

Why celebrate something as simple as hanging your clothes out to dry? It seems like celebrating cooking dinner, taking a walk after work, or other mundane things -- and that might be the point. We seem to have lost touch with some of the more basic functions of living, to the point that they seem odd or even threatening.

Take the simple clothes line. Although sun-dried clothes seem as nonthreatening and wholesome as possible, there are still suburbs and subdivisions that discourage or even disallow hanging clothes out to dry. Reasons typically center around property values, which is something I've never understood. A clothes line itself is not particularly unattractive or even particularly obtrusive, and to me it is an amenity that adds to the value rather than subtracts.

And while I understand that it is unattractive to see a neighbor's clothes hang outside day after day, in the same way Christmas lights in March are annoying, I think the problem lies more in a mistaken belief that possession of a washer and drier indicates affluence. I'm here to say it does nothing of the sort.

It is pretty easy to understand. Until the 1940s at the earliest, most people hung their laundry on a clothes line, and laundry day, even with the early automatic washers, was still a chore. But there was a poetry and a sense of community to it: everyone, from farm to urban apartment, hung their laundry out to dry, and often the birth of a baby was "announced" via the diapers that appeared on the line.

Once post-war consumption made a washer and drier a symbol of the American Dream (along with a car in the garage, a tract home, and a lawn mower to take care of that postage stamp lawn), hanging clothes out to dry meant being a bit behind the times, perhaps a bit poor. And I would imagine that the sense of poverty correlated with what you hung on the line. It is easy to justify hanging sheets outside for that summery smell, and they are relatively attractive, but hang underwear outside and you mark yourself as perhaps not having a drier and, just maybe, not fully participating in the American Dream.

Well, I have an American Dream too, and it includes keeping as much of my money for myself and my family as possible. It includes the luxury of taking time out of my day to stand in the sun with a basket of clean clothes that I snap across the line and pin while I soak up some Vitamin D and some fresh air. It includes the freedom to admit, yes, we wear underwear -- and we wash it regularly too. (Aren't you glad?)

A Pumpkin Pie Worth Leaving Tennessee For

Prepping 101: What is Prepping?

Prepping is, essentially, preparing for situations that might take you temporarily or permanently out of contact with the resources that typically support your lifestyle, such as grocery stores, gas stations, cell service, heating oil, or the electrical/power grid. If you spend an afternoon searching for web sites dedicated to prepping, you will discover that people prep for all sorts of potential emergencies, including but not limited to:

- Weather-related disasters, like blizzards, hurricanes, and floods
- Economic concerns, ranging from personal job-loss to full-scale global economic collapse
- Political disasters, ranging from localized protests to governmental breakdown
- Energy-related disasters, which can be as "minor" as a local power outage or as major as grid collapse from an electromagnetic pulse
- Any change in resource availability that might require you to be more self-sufficient than usual

Now, with all due respect to my prepping colleagues online, I must warn you that if you do decide to spend the afternoon hunting for prepping web sites online, it will probably scare the snot out of you at first. Some of the best-prepared among us seem to have every contingency covered: They own rural property in an undisclosed location on which they have a few acres for garden and livestock, a water filtration system, back-up generators and communications equipment, and their choice of ways to defend it all. Truly, these folks are all set with the prepper basics of "beans, bullets, and Band-aids."

On the other hand, most of the rest of us are guilty of lapses in judgement that could be very harmful in the wrong situation. I know that I have occasionally ventured out in the winter wearing peep-toe heels and with a quarter-tank of gas in the car. What if a snow storm hit and I got caught in a snow drift? What if I had to transport a family member or colleague with a medical emergency?

Being able to be independent in a tough situation is part of the reason we all want to live more sustainably. And sometimes, buying a few extra Band-aids is a good first step.

A Pumpkin Pie Worth Leaving Tennessee For

Prepping 101: Garden Crop Selection for Storage

For many of us, February is the time to place our garden seed orders and get our seedlings started. That makes this a great time to think about the choices we make regarding our garden plants and the ability we have to make those veggies last throughout the year.

Most of us make our decisions on what to plant based on what we like to eat and what we can reasonably grow on our property and in our microclimate. These are important concerns. But, for those of you starting your prepping adventure, I encourage you to think about how you will preserve those veggies for winter use and whether you are making choices that could get you through an emergency of short, medium, or even extended term.

Some of the choices I make:

Veggies that Extend the Season: Lettuces, chard, and other leafy greens are natural season extenders, growing well in even frosty conditions either under row covers, in a pop-up greenhouse, or in a planter in your sunniest window. While these products don't keep well and aren't very high in calories, they will give you a much-needed burst of vitamins in your diet if you are cut off from grocery stores and living on your pantry supplies. Radishes and sprouts will do the same and have the advantage of maturing quickly.

- Buy: High-nutrient greens like Swiss chard, spinach, mustard, and other specialty greens. Try to get some heat-tolerant and some cold-tolerant varieties. Also order your favorite radish and some sprouting seeds, like broccoli or onions.

Veggies/Fruits to Freeze: I tend to think of the freezer as life support for my garden produce. Obviously, any kind of grid collapse is going to drastically shorten the life of food in your freezer. On the other hand, freezing is very easy and frozen food items can serve as pretty easy insurance against wildly fluctuating food prices such as those that might be found in an economic upheaval.

Because I have a small freezer, I use my freezer space for meat and for fruits and veggies that freeze better than they can or dry, like berries and shredded zucchini. I also tend to freeze green beans and sliced carrots, even though these will can well.

- Buy: Berry plants and bushes, and summer squash seeds.

Veggies/Fruits to Water Bath Can: The majority of my food preservation each season is done with a water bath canner, which is very easy to learn to use and is very scalable; you can put up a single pint jar or a whole canner full of quarts with relative ease. Water bath canners are intended to preserve high-acid products, so I use mine to put up jams, preserves, pickles, and tomatoes.

- Buy: Tomatoes for various uses, including paste tomatoes (gives sauces a thickness and richness) and slicers (make great juice in addition to being fabulous raw). Order cucumbers and zucchini for pickles and relishes. Also put in a few berry plants and bushes.

Veggies to Pressure Can: Pressure canning is for low-acid fruits and vegetables, and I won't lie: it is more of a production than water-bath canning. Nonetheless, it is the only way to make some foods into a shelf-stable product. In addition to canning stock and meats, pressure canning is the natural way to preserve some relatively high-energy veggies like corn and beans.

- Buy: Corn if you have space for more than four rows (for pollination purposes, according to Midwestern lore). Also, order the highest-yield beans you can find.

Veggies/Herbs to Dry: Drying is one of the oldest forms of food preservation, and, in a pinch, you can make a solar dryer if you find yourself off the grid. I dry tomatoes and some berries, plus a wide variety of culinary and medicinal herbs. If you can grow nothing else, I highly recommend that you find room for some herb plants and dry your extra for winter; herbs carry a number of healthy phytochemicals that we are only beginning to understand, and the extra pop of flavor could make a diet of pantry supplies much more

A Pumpkin Pie Worth Leaving Tennessee For

palatable.

- Buy: Seeds or plants of herbs that dry well, including basils, oregano, marjoram, thyme, sage, and rosemary. Many of these will also weather the winter in a pot, so you may not have to dry very much to guarantee your supply. Dried tomatoes stay dry and stable if you tuck them in your freezer.

Veggies to Cellar: Finally, some of the foods that we most associate with winter have this connotation because they store well without much preservation effort. Winter squash, potatoes, onions, and carrots all will keep for several months in a cool spot in your house. These crops are the backbone of your prepping, because they will provide enough calories, mass, and satisfying mouth-feel to round out a meal or extend more expensive foods like meat, dairy, and grain.

- Buy: Seeds for carrots and winter squash; starts for potatoes (seed potatoes) and onions. Grow as much as you have room for.

Prepping 101: Readiness Self-Audit

Whether you consider yourself a "prepper" or not, it is a good idea to periodically take stock of your dependence on outside resources and construct a plan for making do with less. This is not an instant fix; instead, think of it as a way to check in with yourself. Find the problems in your preparation, then try to fix them and see where you are in 6 months.

1. **Income:** You don't need to be on the government payroll to experience a sudden drop in income. Mr. FC&G and I are both self-employed, and we experience the end of a major project or the loss of a client fairly regularly. Go through your income streams now (don't forget interest, dividends, part-time jobs, etc.) and see where you are most vulnerable. Try to come up with alternate income streams that may be more insulated from the threats that could harm your main income. For example, we have two Etsy stores and a RedBubble store that won't make us rich, but that aren't in our primary vertical industries of writing, teaching, and manufacturing.

2. **Outflow:** Take a top-line view of your expenditures, and rank what you would omit first, second, third, etc., if your income was cut. As I mentioned, we have done this sort of thing so regularly that we don't even have to have a discussion to know that a slowdown in income means no more dinners out, no recreational shopping, and more meals that stretch the meat and rely on vegetables from the garden.

3. **Make it yourself:** As you run out of things or pay bills this week, ask yourself what you could make yourself and what is "mission critical." To take an example, I know that if our income is cut, I will be baking any cookies and treats we want to eat. However, I can't make fluoride toothpaste, so that remains on the mission critical list. I know that I can heat the house in the fall with the wood stove, but I also know that I need to shut off a few rooms in order to maximize the heating we get out of the wood we've cut.

4. **Plan to DIY:** The companion to making things yourself is to be prepared to do so. I know that I will occasionally try to save money

A Pumpkin Pie Worth Leaving Tennessee For

by baking most of our baked goods, so I stock up on organic flour when it is on special, and buy eggs from pasture-raised chickens at the farmer's market. I also freeze organic butter if I've picked up a couple of extra pounds. What can you stock up on when you're feeling flush that will help you weather a storm?

5. **Be proud:** Once you complete your audit, don't let yourself think of periodic downturns as deprivation or as something you shouldn't have to suffer. These things stink, but it is great to know how self-sufficient you can be. Be proud of taking charge of your life when things are tough, and the good times should be smooth sailing!

Prepper Dress Rehearsal

So, all the good "prepper" books and web sites tell you to be sure to practice with your gear once in a while so you are ready for emergencies. It seems that Mr. FC&G and I run a dress rehearsal every couple of years, whether we mean to or not. One of our most trying lasted 11 days.

It started when we began to lose power to certain parts of the house. The local tree trimmer was working near the power lines, and we naturally assumed something had been hit or dislodged, and we waited until they were finished to call the power company.

Well, the power company came out and said that our 50 year old meter box (unsurprisingly) had taken some damage over the years, and it needed replaced. And then they unhooked all the power to the house and said to give them a call when it was fixed and took off.

So, while Mr. FC&G did the repairs (thank heavens for marrying an electrical engineer!) and we waited for an inspection, we've were living rough. But along the way, we got the "opportunity" to test our preps. Some lessons:

1. It's always the first world problems that get you.
If unplugging the house meant that the entire world were unplugged, we'd have had a much easier time of it. Most of our anxiety involved running a generator to drive, in part, the computers and internet access we would need to work our jobs. Our second problem was running the refrigerator and freezer. I've been in the process of converting more of my food storage efforts to pressure-canned food for this very reason, but our expensive meat from the CSA requires us to keep running that freezer so we don't take a loss.

2. Thank heavens for the fireplace insert.
I used to hate the look of a fireplace insert until I weathered a few power outages around here. Then, I started loving the fact that I could heat the lower level main room and even cook meals on the thing. If you have a largely-decorative fireplace, I'd say a stove insert

is one of the best things you can buy.

3. Your gear is not irrelevant.
Every time I buy prepper gear, I feel profoundly stupid. But every time I have to live without power, I'm grateful. We got out the small cast iron skillet (the large one is theoretically packed safely away in the garage in some location that we can't remember!) and the two-cup tea pot. That made things a lot more bearable.

4. I'm just putting it out here: you need more underwear.
I've wanted to buy some "travel" underwear for a while. You know: the easy-wash, quick-dry stuff you can take on vacation and wash up each evening. I figure, I'm getting tired of packing 20 pairs of undies to take a week long trip to Key West (hey, don't judge...), and 5 really washable pairs would take up less room. After spending this week waiting for a sunny-ish day to wash my unmentionables, this has risen to the top of my list.

Jennifer Patterson Lorenzetti

In Praise of a Clover-Filled Yard

My father has a wonderful story about his grandfather, who we called Pop.

When my Dad was building his first house, Pop told him that he should be sure that he mixed plenty of clover in with the grass seed when he seeded the lawn. According to Pop, the clover would "sweeten" the soil, which was a desirable thing to have happen.

When did we start hating clover in our lawns? Pop was right, you know. Clover is one of the crops that fixes nitrogen in the soil, making it easier for other nitrogen-loving plants to grow. In fact, we are often happy to see some clover creep into our garden, although we usually have to get rid of it to make room for veggies. However, when we do, we use the hoe and cut it off at the surface, leaving those nitrogen-filled root rhizomes in place.

Clover is pretty, too. Remember picking your mother a bouquet of clover and bringing it into the house? I sure do. I loved to follow those slender stems down to the ground and picking the fluffy little white flowers, which Mom would always put in a special tiny vase (which I believe was a crystal toothpick holder). And I spent countless summers looking for a four-leaf clover. If you have kids, you should have at least one huge patch of clover just for the entertainment value.

And the bees! We all know we've had problems in this country with colony collapse and a lack of bees to pollinate our fields and gardens. Growing a special "bee and butterfly" garden of flowers is great, but if you also let the clover grow in your yard, you will attract bees like crazy. In fact, we have one special patch of clover just outside the garden that we tend to "forget" to mow about every other time, and it attracts bees to the flowers. From there, it is a short hop over to the cucumbers, zucchini, and tomatoes, and I regularly find bees nestled in the veggie flowers. Yes, I get stung about once a year, but it is generally from a bee that I've stepped on, which seems fair to me. The bees that are already happily gorging in the veggie flowers

A Pumpkin Pie Worth Leaving Tennessee For

usually leave me alone if I do likewise, and they tend to be docile, sated, and amenable to a gentle brush of the hand to move them if I really need to get into that plant.

Finally, clover is a very economical kind of ground cover. Unlike grass, clover simply doesn't grow very high, so the more patches of clover you have in your yard, the less frequently you have to mow and the easier the job is. We have one side of our yard that is currently about half covered with clover, and it is the easiest section to mow and the one that needs it the least.

Pop was right: in so many ways, clover makes the yard sweet.

Jennifer Patterson Lorenzetti

The Myth of the Extra Tomato

So it's happened again. I mentioned the number of tomato plants I put in, and a well-meaning, generous soul has responded by suggesting a charity that I could donate my "extra tomatoes" to.

This isn't the first time I've heard this. Every year, one or two people have a local charity or food bank that they would like me to send my garden produce to. In general, I think it is a lovely idea. I like the idea of helping those in need have access to fresh, organic vegetables instead of packaged crap, and I may very well decide to make a donation of vegetables as I see fit.

The problem I'm having is this idea of the "extra" tomato. I have never, at any point of my life or at any success level of my garden, looked at my tomato crop and said, "I have no use for these." So, I've set out to attempt to prove or disprove the existence of the "extra" tomato in a scientific fashion.

Hypothesis: There is such a thing as an extra tomato in the FC&G universe.

Proof:
There are 52 weeks in the year. Let's say we don't eat tomato products for four of those weeks, which typically accounts for the period during which all we eat is cucumbers while we wait for the tomatoes to ripen.

Let us further assume that ripe tomato season lasts for eight weeks. During that time, the plants need to produce at least six tomatoes per day to feed the two of us; I can eat that many slicers by myself each day, but let's assume that Mr. FC&G and I each have one Capresse salad per day made of three sliced tomatoes, basil, and cheese, which is not unusual at all.

Then, let's look at how much canned and dried tomato product we would consume if rationing were not an issue. We would easily drink a quart of tomato juice each day, for a total of seven quarts a week.

A Pumpkin Pie Worth Leaving Tennessee For

Then, we would use a certain amount of chili sauce, salsa, dried tomatoes, crushed tomatoes, and plain tomato sauce in our cooking. For ease of calculation, let's say that we would consume eight quarts of tomato products per week.

8 quarts = 2 gallons per week
2 gallons per each of 40 weeks = 80 gallons of tomato products

Therefore, my tomato plants need to produce 80 canned or dried gallons of tomatoes in addition to the 336 slicers we will be eating fresh.

Lest you think that the bottleneck will occur at the canning end, let me point out that I have a 7 quart large canner and a 7 pint small canner. I can do two batches a day in each of those with no problem; I'm a writer who works from home, and I have no fewer than four laptop computers that can move easily. I can spend August in the kitchen.

Let's assume, again for ease of math, that I can two batches totaling 10 quarts on each of five days during each week in August.

10 quarts x 2 batches x 5 days = 100 quarts, or 25 gallons

So, during the month of August, I have the capacity to can 100 gallons of tomato products if need be.

Now, I have great hopes for my tomato plants, but I don't believe for a second that they are going to produce 80 to 100 gallons of canned tomato product.

Hypothesis disproven.
There is no such thing as an "extra" tomato.

Jennifer Patterson Lorenzetti

It's Time to Join a CSA!

If you believe in sustainable living and supporting your local farmers, a CSA is a great way to make your support tangible.

CSA stands for "community supported agriculture." Think of it as Kickstarter for meat and veggies. You purchase a "subscription" for a particular period of time, and once a month (or once a week, maybe), you receive a delivery of farm products that you've specified.

In summer, many farms sell subscriptions to vegetable CSAs, which are a great option for those who don't veggie garden for themselves. You'll pay a certain amount up front, and then once a week or so, you'll go to a pick-up point (maybe at a farmers' market) and get whatever the farmer has harvested in the past couple of days. If it is a good veggie year, you may get more; if it isn't, you may get less. And you may get some veggies you don't normally buy, which is fun.

What we belong to, however, is a meat CSA. I want to talk you through that process as a consumer, because it is a bit different, and I'll admit I felt a little confused at first until I got the hang of it. Now, I wouldn't consider any other way of stocking my freezer!

1. Twice a year, we are asked for a subscription payment and the "level" of our support. We pay around $180 for a six month period, during which we receive 5 lbs. of ground beef and pork sausage each month. That works out to about $6 per pound, which is fantastic for animals raised with a sustainable rotational grazing method on a small farm that uses organic farming methods. I know that Mr. FC&G and I are minimizing exposure to chemicals like glyphosate and getting all the healthy goodness of meat from animals raised in pastures rather than on a CFO. And because I've seen the farm with my own eyes and look the farmer in the face at least once a month, I have a level of trust I wouldn't have otherwise.

2. Each month, our farmer emails us a reminder of our pick-up

point. For us, it's a set time on a certain day in a certain parking lot. Other customers will pick up at farmers' markets the farmer goes to.

3. We also receive a discount on other farm products, and I can tell the farmer by email what I want: eggs, pork chops, roasts, or the like. So I know I have a set quantity of the basic meat we need each month, and then I can tailor our other purchases to my budget and our needs. Grilling season means time for some of his yummy pasture-raised pork chops. I also put in an order for some whole chickens to be harvested later in the summer, so he knows how many animals he needs to raise.

4. That's the big benefit. The farmer gets some up-front payment to help him buy and raise expensive animals, and I get a measure of certainty about how much meat I'll have each month and the quality I can expect. I also know that the meat I'm getting is very fresh, sometimes only days after harvest.

I encourage you to look into the various CSA options available in your area, especially meat CSAs if you are a meat eater. For two people, that five pounds of meat each month are plenty to feed one meat-eater and one "flexitarian," and we feel good about making sure that we're supporting a family farm that treats its animals and the humans who consume them in the most kind, humane, and healthy way possible.

Jennifer Patterson Lorenzetti

Being Sustainable When Things are Going Well

Writing in the sustainable living space, I know that nothing sparks interest in these types of ideas like an economic downturn. Sustainability overlaps nicely with frugality, and people often turn to publications like this for ways to save money when work is a little light.

But what do you do when things are going well?

I'll admit, I've had some days when I wanted to hire a housekeeper, pick up take-out instead of cooking, and forget both the recycling and the gardening. I'm just occasionally that busy. But I don't want to abandon my basic beliefs in managing resources responsibly. So, in case you are in a similar position, here are some of my techniques for practicing sustainability when you are happily busy:

1. Make it count
I still make our laundry soap. Yes, making a big batch takes about 20 minutes, what with grating the soap (and Mr. FC&G tends to do that), but the batch lasts about six months and saves us quite a bit on laundry detergent costs, to say nothing of keeping plastic bottles out of the landfill and reducing transportation costs. It's a good project to prioritize, no matter how busy we are.

On the other hand, I rarely rebatch soap unless I'm really looking for something to do. The savings is comparatively little, and the project yields fairly little soap. That project can wait.

2. Save time for the time-savers
No matter how busy the week is going to be, we still save one weekend day to cook a fairly big meal with as many of the trimmings as we can make. Not only does a home cooked meal save us money and allow us to eat more locally, it throws off leftovers that can often get us through several days during the week. That makes it less likely that we will succumb to a restaurant meal, even when things are feeling financially healthy enough that that isn't a worrisome hit to the budget.

3. Spend responsibly

If you have a little extra money and feel like you can spend on some luxuries, spend responsibly. Buy from local, small businesses. Look for organic, cruelty-free, and fair trade products. Patronize businesses that you want to see around for years to come. They will thank you, and they may even return the favor!

Jennifer Patterson Lorenzetti

Chapter 3: Finances

Jennifer Patterson Lorenzetti

A Pumpkin Pie Worth Leaving Tennessee For

Gardening, Food Preservation, and the Freelance Life

While my family's interest in home food preservation is a step toward living sustainably, it is also a natural outgrowth of the fact that we are both small business owners. Read any article on freelancing, and you almost certainly will see the advice to sock a chunk of your income away in savings to guard against the inevitable unevenness in workload. But what most people don't tell you is that you also have to have mechanisms in place to lower your outflow of cash when times are rough. For us, gardening and food preservation help bridge any gaps.

I keep a fairly obsessive tally of the retail value of my garden harvests. Even in the worst years, the garden more than pays for itself, giving us fresh, organically-grown produce that has a retail value far above our investment in seeds and plants. Obviously, this decreases our food bill overall by that amount while we eat healthy, fresh food.

By preserving some of this bounty (and supplementing from the farmers' market), we are also guarding against income fluctuations in non-harvest months. If neither of us are having a particularly productive February, for example, we know we can cut back our grocery budget and still eat well by relying on our stocks of tomato sauce, chili sauce, soup stock, jams and preserves, and relishes, all of which add nutrition and interest to very inexpensive meals. Some of our preserved food, like my bread and butter pickles, are also popular gifts in our family.

It is unconventional advice, but I swear by it. If you are contemplating a freelance/small business career, you simply must garden as much as your property allows and preserve food to the best of your abilities. Your budget and your business will thank you.

Jennifer Patterson Lorenzetti

The Bricks and Mortar Method to Financial Stability

Like many writers in the sustainable homemaking space, I'm guilty of writing more about saving and extending resources than I am about gaining more, particularly when it comes to money. Oh, sure, I write about how to get more produce out of your garden or more fleece when you go to the fabric store, but I don't spend as much time as I might on how to make more money. This is an oversight on my part, because part of the sustainability equation is increasing your resources.

Think of it this way: "sustainability" means nothing more or less than a system that can keep going for the foreseeable future because its rate of use of its resources does not exceed how quickly the resources are made available. If we were talking about using our cars, we would say that our driving habits were sustainable if we could make it to all of our commitments and errands with the gas we can put in our tanks on our gas budget. When gas prices go up, we either have to decrease our driving or increase our gas budget to keep the system sustainable.

The same is true with your income, and for this, I like to think of my approach as the "bricks and mortar" system of making money. Full disclosure: I am speaking from the perspective of a small business owner, but I think those of you with full-time or part-time employment can adapt this system as well. Certainly, I use this thought process no matter where my income comes from.

Your income derives from two sources. First are the "bricks." These are the building blocks of your financial fortune, and you can't build your financial fortress without them. For me, each metaphorical brick is a large project; each brick represents a commitment to a large chunk of work that will pay well. I need to be sure that I have a steady stream of bricks coming in, so for me that means cultivating good anchor clients who will feed me a reasonably steady stream of work over the course of a year.

If you are employed full-time, your bricks might be your biweekly paychecks or your base number of hours you are scheduled to work

A Pumpkin Pie Worth Leaving Tennessee For

each pay period. An adjunct professor might think of each class she teaches as a brick. The point is, your bricks are your large chunks of income that are more or less dependable.

This is where most of us stop, but the strength of your fortress lies not only with your bricks, but with your mortar. To really have a sustainable income, you need to fill in the gaps with other projects and income sources that can help you hold things together. For me, a lot of my "mortar" comes from my smaller clients (income-wise). These are the clients, some long-term and some one-time, who send me smaller projects or one-off opportunities. When I feel like I have a gap between "brick" projects, you can be sure I make the rounds of old and new clients who might have some "mortar" available.

My mortar is also made up of extras from my "brick" projects, like add-on projects from clients who might be having a seasonal rush or need extra help. Also, I get my mortar from my Etsy and RedBubble shops. You could easily do likewise by picking up a part-time holiday job, selling some garden produce, or doing any number of other interesting short-term projects, like becoming a poll worker on election day.

Jennifer Patterson Lorenzetti

My Sustainable Car

In late 1997, I took delivery of my brand new car. I was so thrilled to get my navy blue sedan; I've always loved four-door cars (in obvious rebellion against my strictly-two-door parents), and I so much wanted a car in my favorite color.

In the intervening years, she has served me well, lasting until the day I retired her to the garage, and I now keep her as just as a fair weather, pleasure-only vehicle. That said, having the extra vehicle has saved my hide a time or two.

Our culture expects consumers to get a new car every two to five years, which may be good for the auto industry but is bad for your pocketbook and your sustainable lifestyle. A couple of the benefits of keeping your car way past the trade-in expectation are:

No car payments for years: To be honest, I wrote a check for my car, so I've never had car payments. God willing and knock wood, my plan is to never go into long-term debt for anything smaller than a house. But even if you take five years to pay off a new car, keeping it for 15 would mean a whole decade without payments. If you put even half of that money into a savings account, think of how much you would have. For example, let's say I typically budget $400 a month for a car payment. If I spend a decade without making that payment and save half of it each month, I would amass $24,000 before interest. That's a good way toward another new car, a room addition on your house, or a year's tuition at a decent college.

Safety from knowing your vehicle: My car and I have been together so long that I know if something is wrong just by how the engine sounds. I can tell how fast I'm going from the vibration of the seat (although I do check the speedometer). I know exactly how big of a parking space I can fit into and still comfortably open the doors, and I know how much room to allow for stopping on dry pavement. This all translates into better driving.

So, how can you make your car last for a decade and a half or more?

A Pumpkin Pie Worth Leaving Tennessee For

My method won't work for everyone, but here's what has made my car into my lifelong companion:

I drive very little: OK, this tip will not work for those of you in certain geographic situations, but I have always lived my life around avoiding driving. It isn't that I am purposely being miserly; it is just that driving bores me to tears. I've never been one of those people who can't wait to slide behind the wheel; even as a teenager, I thought cars were transportation, not entertainment. Therefore, when I chose jobs as a single woman, I would only consider jobs located within about 20 minutes of where I wanted to live. If a job would require a 30 minute commute, I would either turn down the job or consider moving. I just don't want to spend my life in a car, no matter how cute it is. In fact, one of the top motivations for starting my own business and working from home was that I could go days without getting into a car, except maybe for a brief shopping or gym errand.

I drive so little that, years ago when I did a calculation of how many years it would take me to recoup the cost differential between a new traditional car and a new hybrid car in fuel savings, I came up with something like 20 years. Things have certainly changed, with lower relative prices of hybrids and higher gas prices, but by keeping to a very moderate driving schedule, I can drive what I want with no guilt.

My Dad is a car guy: Papa FC&G is a car guy extraordinaire. He shows a car, and he has always enjoyed detailing and working on cars. He is the only man I know (but not the only one *he* knows!) who thinks Q-tips are a car detailing tool. I once bought him a glorified dental mirror so he could check the undersides of engine parts for dirt and grime. So trust me, he doesn't let me forget my routine maintenance, and he makes very good suggestions about mechanics to use if I have a problem. Not everyone has a car guy father, but I'll bet most of you have a friend who can give advice (if you don't care for such things yourself). Also, it helps to keep that maintenance record that came in your original car manual filled out, and pay attention to such things as suggested maintenance at given mileages. Dropping a couple or a few hundred bucks once in a while is a small price to pay to keep your car running well.

I protect my car: This car has never sat out overnight (except for very occasional emergencies), but even before I had this car, I always tried to find a way to shelter my vehicle. At first, I did have to leave my car out, but I tried to park in relatively sheltered locations overnight (I got very good at knowing which way storm fronts blew in over certain apartment complexes and which parking spots seemed to get less snow). As soon as it was financially practical, I rented a carport, and later, a garage.

Even if you can't garage your car, I can tell you one way to protect your vehicle that everyone can do: Set a rule that NO ONE eats in the car. Yes, that means you, the car owner, too. I hate the smell of fast food that lingers in a car, and I hate the chance of spills on upholstery and greasy fingerprints on the steering wheel, although I am always guilty of there being mascara and lipstick on my steering wheel from me touching my face while driving. Growing up, it was a hard-and-fast rule in our house that if anyone needed to eat or drink anything, we stopped the car and got out for that to happen, either at a restaurant or a rest stop. This is my biggest rule for my car today, and it has the added benefit of making us all a little more mindful about our eating. If you have to stop to eat, you may as well make good choices about what you are consuming. And maybe you don't really need to consume anything at all.

Do some detailing once in a while: Papa FC&G is going to laugh at me for this, because I am not nearly as good as he is, but I will say that it is a good idea to get out once in a while to wash your car, vacuum the inside, and clean the various surfaces and windows. You'll feel good about your car's condition, and it will keep the finish from being damaged by road salt and the like. (Pro tip: Never use a slick cleaner like some of the tire polishes to clean your gear shift, steering wheel, or foot pedals, because they could cause your hands or feet to slip off at an inopportune moment).

So there you have it. When I took delivery of my car, I planned to replace her at 10 years or 60,000 miles, whichever came first. As of this publication, I have had her for over 21 years and have just under 61,000. I no longer want to replace her, although I wouldn't mind giving her a cute little playmate. My car has lasted with a shiny finish and a bounce in her step.

Jennifer Patterson Lorenzetti

Chapter 4: News and Issues

Jennifer Patterson Lorenzetti

A Pumpkin Pie Worth Leaving Tennessee For

Lessons from Living on a Food Stamp-Sized Budget

Many bloggers run a "food stamp challenge" for themselves in an attempt to better understand the food situation of those in poverty, and some conclude that it is government subsidies that are critical to the good health of these citizens. This may or may not be your conclusion, but I thought it would be interesting to compare my own food experience with that of the food stamp budget to see what complexities emerge that might make this problem more than just a simple problem of governmental transfer payments.

I generally keep track of the money Mr. FC&G and I spend at grocery stores and farmers' markets. I make no effort to restrict us to items that would be allowed under the food stamp program, so along with our pasta and potatoes, these figures tend to include the odd bottle of injector cleaner, an area rug, or a grinder of Himalayan sea salt. For the first four full months of 2012, we had the following totals:

January: $557.87
February: $354.82
March: $308.55
April: $466.68
Overall Average: $421.98

The SNAP budget for a family of two at that point was $367 per month, so you will note that for two of our four months, we actually spent less on groceries than the SNAP program would have allowed. The average expenditure puts us just $55 over the SNAP budget, so we are not eating at the poverty level, but we are certainly not overspending for a DINK household with two healthy incomes.

So what are the complicating factors?

Our list here doesn't include restaurant meals, which probably average one per week. On the other hand, these were four pretty good months to choose, because Mr. FC&G was not travelling for business and doing a lot of eating out on per diem reimbursements.

These totals are more or less what it took to feed us.

We were not eating badly. We eat hormone-free cheese; local, free-range eggs; local, grass-fed beef, and free range chicken. I suspect the SNAP program administrators would blanch at the $6.50 I pay for a pound of grass-fed stew meat. We make extremely healthy choices.

On the other hand, we have the ability to make those choices. Looking back on my grocery tallies, there were days that we went to three different grocery stores and a farmers' market to get our food. We can drive anywhere we wish to source our food, and we can (and do) choose to spend up when we are at a farmers' market, because we want to keep our local providers in business.

We have the money to stock up. Part of this tally includes a stock-up spree on organic vanilla that Mr. FC&G undertook when reading of threats to global vanilla supply. We regularly stock up on pantry items like flour, honey, olive oil, and other things when we see a good price, whether that throws us over the SNAP budget each month or not.

We have a garden. Although these four months were certainly the most garden-free of the year, we still were eating canned and dried foods from last summer, and our monthly outlay drops as I start bringing in fresh produce. We have the land and the tools and the knowledge to produce our own food.

So what does this mean? Well, for me it indicates that we must do a better job using space, particularly urban spaces like rooftops, to allow more people to grow and produce food to live within a budget. One of the differences between the experience of the poor historically versus now is that it used to be common for residents of tenement buildings to keep chickens for meat and eggs. Although I can't imagine how that must have smelled in apartments with too many people and too few windows that opened onto air shafts, it points out that we have required the poorest members of our communities to be divorced from the sources of their food. Changing the SNAP budget one way or the other won't make anyone's life more sustainable.

A Pumpkin Pie Worth Leaving Tennessee For

I believe that caring people across the spectrum look at the problem and propose a variety of ways to solve it. However, my take-away from my analysis is that it is not just a question of budget, it is a question of time, knowledge, and ability to pursue procurement of the kinds of foods we want to eat to stay healthy. When we have those tools, we can even throw the occasional choice from the automotive section in there.

Walkability = Sustainability

Recently, I came across coverage of Walk Score, an online neighborhood-assessment service that uses a proprietary algorithm to score an address in terms of "walkability." In general, it takes into account the viability of doing daily errands on foot, so densely-populated urban areas, which might have a variety of grocers, book stores, coffee shops, and yoga studios within a small radius, score pretty highly on the 1-100 scale. Not surprisingly, rural and suburban areas score poorly.

In general, the score tallies with what I know of the neighborhoods I am most familiar with. My beloved Oxford, Ohio, where I went to college, has an average walkability score of 59, and it is easy to see why. If you live in town and work at the university, you probably park your car in the garage and only take it out to visit out-of-town friends and relatives. Everything is walkable in that town, and the university creates a demand for a number of bars, restaurants, theaters, and shops that would not otherwise be present in a town of that size. In Oxford, I have generally found it more difficult to drive than to walk, and if I lived in the highly-rural "exurbs" of the town and worked at the university, I would drive to a parking place, park, and then walk all day long until time to go home.

Similarly, my also-beloved Key West rates an average of 70. Again, the town is actually more difficult to drive in than to bike in or walk, and the compact size of the island compared with the demand for amenities posed by tourists means that the only reasonable way to get around is to walk or bike. I have not done an actual survey, but it would not surprise me to learn that there are more formal and informal places to park a bike than a car.

Home, however, is a different matter, and again I understand why. My house in the suburbs rates a 20. Although I bike a number of errands that others wouldn't, we live in an area in which we have to drive many we need to go, even if the distance is theoretically walkable or bikeable, because the roads are often too dangerous to navigate. We are in the uncomfortable position of having to drive to

A Pumpkin Pie Worth Leaving Tennessee For

the gym.

But I don't know if one's Walk Score is the end-all and be-all of sustainability. Primarily, the Walk Score favors urban areas; if you plan to utilize an outside provider of some sort for all of your needs, from food to entertainment, then you will be happiest in a place with a high Walk Score. In fact, the Walk Score seems to place a high value on amenities in a very small radius, so packing apartments on top of grocers and coffee shops will contribute to a high score.

But if you plan to try to live independently through gardening, using wood for heat, keeping chickens and rabbits, and even hanging your laundry outside, you will probably be happier in a suburb or rural area. Yes, we tend to get in our car every day, but we also walk into our own yard to get a fair amount of our food, and we are able reduce our dependence on others through the use of our land. We also have a house with enough space to run both of our consulting-type businesses, further reducing our need for long commutes. And, should we decline to drive to the gym, we can certainly get all the exercise we want in the form of weeding the garden, chopping wood, mowing the lawn, and flipping compost.

So, my final assessment of Walk Score? It is a good tool for a certain lifestyle, and I definitely would like to see more communities make human-powered commuting easier via bike lanes, pedestrian-friendly sidewalks, and a culture that looks out for people who are not sheltered by cars. But the Walk Score is not a complete proxy for measuring sustainability. That, too, is a lifestyle choice.

Jennifer Patterson Lorenzetti

Gypsies in the Palace, Redux

With the cold weather shutting down many of the "Occupy X" protest sites, it seems the national conversation over how we feel about the 1% is dying down a bit. I'll admit that I am glad, because I think the news coverage on both sides of the issue oversimplifies. On the one hand, becoming fabulously wealthy by working your tail off is part of the American dream and should be honored. On the other hand, becoming fabulously wealthy by behaving in ways that crush the future potential of others is not part of that dream.

But this is not a political column, because I have news for you: If you are reading this blog, you are probably part of the 1%.

According to a study reported on CNN.com, it takes only $34,000 (USD) after taxes for an individual to be among the wealthiest 1% of the world's population. Half of these folks live in the U.S. To put this in perspective, the median global income -- statistically, the global "middle class" -- is $1,225 a year. If you are reading this blog from your own internet connection in a house or apartment on which you can pay the bills, you are almost certainly among the top 5% of the world's population. Feeling rich yet?

This is not to discount the reality of poverty, even in a country like the U.S. or other first world nations. And yes, there are many among us who have lost jobs, lost homes, and are wondering how they will make ends meet right now. I cannot diminish that suffering.
But the statistical analysis reported in the CNN story has some bearing on how we view our sustainable living behavior. I refer back to a short piece I wrote on this in 2010 called "Gypsies in the Palace." I think the point is relevant here as we consider our use of economic as well as environmental resources.

I tend to think of responsible stewardship of resources -- money, food, fuel, time -- in terms of the Jimmy Buffett song "Gypsies in the Palace." In it, Buffett tells the story of going off on tour, leaving his house in the care of two men (one of whom is named "Snake"). The housesitters waste no time shooting the lock off his liquor cabinet

A Pumpkin Pie Worth Leaving Tennessee For

and throwing a clothing-optional party for the neighborhood, especially the attractive women from the nearby condos. When they get a call that Buffett is returning home early, they waste no time shutting down their party and faking a bunch of wholesome industry, including mowing and raking the lawn.

In my original piece, I contend that how we use resources can be likened to housesitting for God. Yes, the homeowner wants you to make yourself comfortable, but throwing a kegger and trashing the house is out of the question.

The same is true as we look at our responsibility as part of the global 1% (or 5% or 10%, or wherever you fall -- statistically, you are probably still pretty lucky). Yes, we should use the resources we need to live our best possible life. And yes, sometimes that means that we will achieve in ways that others cannot, either through hard work or luck of birth or some combination of factors. That's OK.

But the idea behind sustainability is living in a way that is sustainable -- that is, using resources in a way that they will last until they can be replenished. So ask yourself, this new year, if you are being truly responsible with the resources you have been given, or if you need to cut back a bit here or there so that resources of all types are available for you and others to thrive in the long term. For all of us who count ourselves fortunate, there is surely a place that we could behave more conservatively.

It is all a matter of perspective whether we believe we are fortunate or deprived. That's why I chose the photo above. If you thought that was for a charity food line, perhaps from the Depression, think again. I took that photo in a large bakery in San Francisco. It literally is the sign for the line to buy sourdough baguettes, which we ate in the company of throngs of statistically very wealthy people, especially when viewed from a global perspective. How you see things depends a great deal on context.

So, metaphorically speaking, I think we global housesitters should feel free to enjoy the property that we're watching. We just might not want to take our behavioral cues from friends named Snake.

Of Coffee and Avocados

Most of my philosophy of sustainable living is based on controlling small things. I've told you to plant a single basil plant, eliminate buying cotton balls, and switch to at least one vegetarian meal a week, all to save money and resources. But today I'm going to tell you why that approach has to be taken in balance, and it all comes down to coffee and avocados.

Back in the day, I was part of a marketing research project for a company that I will not name, but which makes some of the best grocery-store-level ground coffee out there. The project sought to figure out why Generation X was eschewing coffee in favor of pop in the mornings as we became adults.

See, the crux of the problem was the generation ahead of us. After a youth spent going to Woodstock and a young adulthood spent at Studio 54 (or the equivalent, for both), they had settled into corporate jobs, and they needed to make some money. And those who sold coffee were getting pretty worried that the next generation was not adopting the all-American habit of a cup or six every morning.

To make a long story somewhat shorter, the findings of the project were that young adults basically needed their coffee to not taste like coffee. We preferred it to taste like hot chocolate or some other highly-flavored drink, and an entire industry of flavored creamers and "gourmet" coffee shops was born. We settled into needing our coffee every morning just like generations before us had done.

But, as the economy experienced inevitable ups and downs and the mortgage market got tough and we were having trouble getting promotions at work, some of that older generation had a brilliant idea: Perhaps we couldn't buy the houses and cars we wanted and fund our retirement plans like we wanted because we were drinking too many coffee-shop lattes. Just start bringing your own brew to work in a thermos, and you'll be just fine! Put that $3 or so you save every day into your IRA or toward your mortgage, and the American

A Pumpkin Pie Worth Leaving Tennessee For

Dream is all yours.

I'm guilty of this too. I give that kind of advice, and I will continue to tell you to make small changes because they allow you to take control of your life in a very tangible way. And I think I have about two coffee shop coffees a year, preferring the savings realized from my own percolator.

But, if you're struggling financially, chances are it isn't because of the coffee.

I say this because of an annoying trend I see in the media castigating Millennials for buying too much avocado toast and saying that they will never move out of their parents' houses because they are buying too many avocados.

Yeah, that's it. We have a generation that we've saddled with student loan debt the size of a mortgage. If they opt to freelance or be small business owners (as many do), they also pay a health insurance premium that is the size of a mortgage. And buying a house (and taking an actual mortgage) is no longer the guaranteed increase in value that it once was. All of these things are political and societal problems that are beyond the scope of this blog.

But I just wanted to say to all the Millennials: Yes, absolutely watch the money you spend on little things. Restaurant meals add up, as do other small expenses. Take control where you can, because you have to handle that mountain of expenses so you can have a shot at a prosperous life. Heck, I'll even tell you to learn to make avocado toast at home so you don't spend the money for someone else to do it.

But don't ever feel guilty for liking a nutritious fruit and taking some pleasure in what you eat. If you are feeling the crunch, it probably isn't due to the avocados

Is Gardening a Subversive Act?

Well, it's summer once again, and the news is full of human interest stories about people being penalized for growing food on their own property. There's the standard array of home owners' associations mandating that people remove front yard gardens and neighborhoods adopting policies that gardens, along with clothes lines, depress the property values. My favorite involved a municipality that declared that the right to grow food was something to be bestowed by the government, and, since the government had not explicitly conferred this right, the area homeowners could not garden.

Gardening, in some places, has become a subversive act. And this is the kind of subversion I can get behind.

Think of it this way. Every time you plant something you can eat, you remove a little of your dependence on corporations that produce and distribute foodstuffs. Every tomato you pick from your garden is a little less reliance on a corporate entity to provide your dinner. It also is a little step toward independence in the form of better health. That tomato, grown your way (organically, if you so desire), brings you the kind of nutrition that might help ward off diseases and disorders, freeing you from reliance on healthcare and pharmaceuticals.

This is not to say that gardening is a fix for "everything that ails ya." Most of us would notice if the food trucks didn't come to our local grocer, and most of us will need to take advantage of medical care, even if we eat nothing but homegrown organic produce and do yoga every day.

But, every bit of your own food you grow is one step toward greater independence and less reliance on the impersonal structures that seem to govern our lives. That's the kind of subversive behavior I encourage.

A Pumpkin Pie Worth Leaving Tennessee For

Lessons Watching Irma from Afar

As you all know by now, I am in love with Key West, so I spent a nail-biting four days watching Hurricane Irma approach and pass over the island. Key West iteslef was mostly spared, although islands in the middle keys were not as lucky.

I've watched everyone pass wisdom around the internet, some of it useless and some of it downright destructive, and it reminds me that we all need a well-thought-out disaster plan well in advance of anything that may hit us. To that end, I thought I'd share a few tips that I have recently read that I thought were particularly helpful. If you have others or can contribute your own experience, please comment!

Additions to Your Disaster Plan

- Plan your "bug out outfit" or "disaster outfit" in advance. Try to come up with something that will handle various temperatures and situations. You may want a pair of quick-dry pants (nylon fishing pants work well in lots of climates) with cargo pockets; for cold weather, you can always add a silk base layer. Consider layering a tank top and an active-wear sweater if you are in a cooler area. Don't forget socks and hiking boots or something that will protect your toes from injury or infection. Break your shoes in ahead of time. Don't forget a hat for both temperature and sun protection.

- Sleep in your evacuation clothes. For disasters that come upon us suddenly, like rising water, you won't have time to get dressed, and no one wants to be on the news wearing undies and a t-shirt, to say nothing of sitting on their own roof that way waiting to be rescued.

- Likewise, pack a bag ahead of time. Make sure you have all of your medications, a knife, a whistle, and some ID in there, in addition to a full water bottle and some portable food, like granola bars. Take a couple of extra pairs of socks and some quick-drying undies, if you have them. Don't forget a flashlight, because you will be saving your phone for communication.

- Along the same lines, keep all of your electronics (like phone, tablet, etc.) fully charged for as long as you maintain power, and have a few external chargers as a backup.

- Even if you don't like social media, get a Facebook account. You don't have to do anything with it, but if you are in a disaster like Irma, you can post your whereabouts and tag family outside the disaster zone to let them know your status and potentially how to send help. Don't forget to set your posts to "public" so they are more easily visible. For all of its security-related downfalls, Facebook seems to have consistently been the one social medium that updates regularly and that is used by all ages, making it a good communication tool in emergency when appropriate.

- Freeze large freezer-type bags of water to stock your chest and fridge freezers. They will help keep the contents cold, and you will have drinkable water as they melt.

- Fill every receptacle with water while you can. Your bathtub and washing machine will hold water for washing and flushing your toilet. Every large pot and jar should hold drinkable water. Remember, you don't have to buy water to have a good supply of it as long as you plan ahead.

A Pumpkin Pie Worth Leaving Tennessee For

Jennifer Patterson Lorenzetti

Chapter 5: Humor

Jennifer Patterson Lorenzetti

A Pumpkin Pie Worth Leaving Tennessee For

Midwest Seasonal Grieving

You might be under the impression that as a Midwesterner writing about sustainability topics, I must be in sync with the seasons. That somehow I find as much magic in a cold, clear night with temps in the teens and snow on the ground as I do in the warmest days of July with the garden just beginning to produce.

You'd be wrong.

No, like many Midwesterners, I go through a process of grieving about every year in the fall, as the days grow shorter and the garden dies off and I'm left with outside clean-up chores done on nippy days. So, for the benefit of those who don't live around here, let me explain to you the process of Midwestern Seasonal Grieving.

Stage One: Denial
"No, it isn't going to get cold yet. Look, it's the end of September and I'm still wearing flip-flops! I still have tomatoes on the vine," we protest. We bravely joke about global warming in line at the bank and grocery store: "Hey, maybe climate change is really a thing! Maybe this is all the colder it's going to get," we claim. We keep hoping that, if the globe really is warming, it might bring the first favorable weather shift that the Midwest has seen in millennia.

Stage Two: Anger
"OMG! It is actually snowing out there! WTF?" we all post on Facebook. Everyone starts trotting out stories of how miserable they are every year during winter. Tales of local drivers who have driven here all their lives yet still can't manage to slow down during a sleet storm are exchanged. Friends who dare to mention or post things about liking snow or enjoying the change of seasons are resoundingly put in their places, along with the snow they so richly deserve.

Stage Three: Depression
Depression, indeed, and it might actually be seasonal depression, which is a real condition that your doctor will give you happy pills to combat. However, if you're a Midwesterner born and bred, you

probably get a certain amount of relief from making everyone around you miserable while you shiver, shake, and sink further into despondency, the light of your mood growing dimmer as the days shorten.

Stage Four: Bargaining
"I'm fine with the cold just as long as it doesn't snow," we say. And then, when Mother Nature laughs, we offer up Christmas, New Years, weekends, or any other day that we don't have to shovel a driveway or get on an icy highway. Periodically, we celebrate a rare 51 degree day by going outside wearing a fleece shirt but no jacket and declaring that the chores we got done through chattering teeth and numbing fingers count as "gardening."

Stage Five: Acceptance
The first seeds that we've planted inside under the grow lights sprout, and we content ourselves with the idea that we are starting the summer garden. We ignore the mounting snow outside, the short tempers in the grocery store, and the puddles that stand under our boots in the entry way. We settle in to wait for the day that we will first take those little seedlings outside to harden off, and life will be worth living again.

A Pumpkin Pie Worth Leaving Tennessee For

Merry Christmas, Or Why The Candy Doesn't Work the First Time

I love sugar. I know that it's more correct these days for those of us writing in the sustainable, "clean food" space to turn up our noses at processed sugars, but I can't help it. I love the stuff. Attempts to control the craving limits my intake, but they never truly eliminate the desire.

I get the craving honestly. Papa FC&G also has what Mr. FC&G calls a "power pancreas," and we both will go to incredible lengths to find the finest examples of dessert. And every year at Christmas while I was growing up, this turned into the desire to make homemade fudge.

Now, I'm not talking about marshmallow-based fudge or any of the so-called "foolproof" recipes, I mean real, boil the sugar and pray it sets up fudge. And every year we'd blow it. The pancreas may be willing, but the ability falls short.

Each year, even though the house was full of cookies, it seemed like the days off of school and work would spur either Papa FC&G or I to say, "let's make fudge!" Mama FC&G would try to pitch in, but while she has much greater cooking skills, she's a salty snack person and does not have the intrinsic love of sugar. Nonetheless, the three of us would gather in the kitchen and try to get cooked fudge to set up.

"Is that a soft ball?" we'd ask. It was a valid question, since none of us had ever succeeded in getting fudge to the actual soft ball stage. We'd drop blob after blob of fudge into a cup of cold water, occasionally making the water colder, occasionally trying to nudge the blob with a spoon to get it to ball up. But it just never happened. Somehow, even a candy thermometer didn't help.

Eventually, we'd declare it "close enough" (never a great idea in candy-making) and pour it into the fudge dish. The dish was a square glass plate with Ulysses S. Grant embossed at the bottom, and poor old U.S. Grant was routinely buttered and made to sit through the insult of having hot fudge poured on his face.

Of course, the fudge didn't set. Oh, we left it on the counter, we put it in the fridge, we left it sit overnight, but to no avail. So finally, the justifications started.

   "We could eat that with a spoon."
   "Yep, it will taste just fine."

And finally Papa FC&G would deliver the coup: "That's ice cream topping!"

And so, every year, we'd give up on cutting the fudge and go at it with a spoon. It tasted just fine, thank you very much.

I thought about this when making maple sugar candy. It took me two tries to turn maple syrup into solid candy, which shouldn't have been hard. But I'm missing the gene that makes me able to turn liquid sugar into solid, and I struggled for an hour until it set up.

I still wound up eating some of it with a spoon. But at least I didn't pour it all over a long-suffering U.S. President before I did so.

A Pumpkin Pie Worth Leaving Tennessee For

I don't know when Christmas stopped being a holiday that took up the last half of December and started being an Olympic decathlon with events like "creative baking," "holiday card design," and "targeted gift purchasing," but every year, the pressure to pull off a spectacular Christmas seems to mount. And, just a reminder, Mr. FC&G and I don't have kids, so we aren't even engaged in the side of things that involves figuring out what the toy of the year is and how to hide it from inquisitive eyes, to say nothing of that super-creepy marketing ploy that is the Elf on the Shelf. No, we just feel your garden variety pressure, and it is getting out of hand.

Now, many others opining about their Christmas tasks are going to blame the pressure on Facebook, with its uncanny ability to catalog all of your friends' most perfect milliseconds of life and throw them in your face at the moment you are about to start hurling bakeware across your kitchen. ("Wait, little Billy, stop and hold that toy from Aunt Beth just so while I get a photo of you with the Christmas tree in the background. That should make all my friends insanely jealous of my perfect life, which, of course, is the true meaning of Christmas!")

No, this pressure goes back to Christmas carols, a fact of which I am now painfully aware since the radio station that I depended upon to play 80s New Wave decided to convert to the city's "Christmas Station" starting the day after Halloween. I swear, if they back this holiday up any further, I'm going to be forced to sing Jingle Bells while I'm cleaning up from the Fourth of July cookout.

Anyway, listen to some of these things:

(There's No Place Like) Home for the Holidays (1954)
I met a man who lives in Tennessee
And he was headin' for
Pennsylvania and some homemade pumpkin pie.

Think about that. The distance between Nashville, TN, and

Harrisburg, PA, is 720 miles, or over 10 hours in the car, not counting rest stops. I don't know about you, but my pumpkin pie, although pretty darn good, isn't worth driving from the neighboring town for, let alone hauling butt for 11 hours in the car. It's tasty, but it always gets that crack down the middle.

Sleigh Ride (1949)
There's a happy feeling nothing in the world can buy
When they pass around the coffee and the pumpkin pie
It'll almost be like a picture print by Currier and Ives.
These wonderful things are the things
We remember all through our lives.

Currier and Ives, people! We're supposed to create a Christmas that is so good that it doesn't just get recorded on our phones but is actually worthy of a lithograph! I can't do that! And again with the pumpkin pie - although, I must say, my coffee is pretty kick-ass, especially if you like your brew strong enough to strip paint off the walls and keep you up for three days.

It's the Most Wonderful Time of the Year (1963)
There'll be parties for hosting
Marshmallows for toasting
And caroling out in the snow.
There'll be scary ghost stories
And tales of the glories
Of Christmases long long ago!

OK, so now I see why we're starting this holiday at Halloween, because that's clearly the only reasonable time to toast marshmallows and tell ghost stories. But tales of the glories? What would you like to hear about? The time that I actually got the fudge to set up on the first try? (And what, exactly, is a "soft ball stage?") See, I'm supposed to throw a Christmas so good that we have guests coming in at all hours, traipsing up and down the street signing carols, and it **still** will pale in comparison to past Christmases, which we will fondly recall. ("I don't know, Jen, this pumpkin pie is good, but it isn't as good as that year you got everyone to come in from Nashville just for a piece.")

A Pumpkin Pie Worth Leaving Tennessee For

So I don't know, folks. These kinds of essays are supposed to end with some cheery pronouncement that "it's all worth it." But I have to go - I need to finish the calligraphy on the envelopes of my Christmas cards and try to take a perfect, soft-focus picture of the Christmas tree to post to Facebook. Then, I apparently need to investigate some new pie recipes, because mine just aren't bringing the crowds to the door.

Mr. and Mrs. FC&G Replace a Sewer Pipe: A Tragedy in Four Acts
Or
How the World's Best Ballroom Dancer Picked My Kitchen Sink

Act I

It all started when we thought we'd gotten lazy about the compost.

Like a lot of DIY sustainability types, we have a compost pile, and that means we have a compost bucket. Now, one really needs to empty that bucket every day, especially during high gardening season, but sometimes you get lazy. So, when we started to smell rotted food in the fall of 2008, we immediately blamed the compost.

We started being vigilant about emptying the bucket every day. Then, it was every time we put a scrap of food in it. Then, it was a thorough washing outside before the empty bucket dared to come back in the house. By the end, we were pretty much carrying individual tomato peels and cores out to the compost pile as soon as they were cut, then sterilizing the compost bucket and sunning it for extra measure. But the smell continued.

Mr. FC&G insisted that the smell wasn't a clogged drain pipe (spoiler: he was right), but I was unconvinced. So, one day I bought a bottle of Draino and dumped it down the non-disposal side of the kitchen sink. I was quickly rewarded with the fresh, chemical smell of Draino wafting through the house every time the AC kicked on.

"See, I fixed it!" I crowed! "Now you can just smell how clean that pipe is."

Mr. FC&G didn't so much react as wilt, visibly, on the spot. "Yeah, that's what I was afraid of," he said.

A Pumpkin Pie Worth Leaving Tennessee For

I will always remember this moment of my life as the last time I was truly innocent about the horrors of home ownership. "Whatever do you mean, my darling husband?" I asked. (I may be remembering that moment a bit better than it actually was.)

"You didn't clean the pipe. The sewer pipe from the kitchen sits on top of the ductwork that returns to the HVAC system. We have a pipe that is leaking, and you just leaked Draino into the air ducts."

After a bit calm discussion (or else I'm intentionally misremembering that part too), two things became clear: First, if the heat had been on instead of the AC, I could have sent a stream of Draino into the heater, and, second, our sewer pipe was located in our slab.

"What do you mean, 'in the slab?' Is there a crawl space?"

"No," Mr. FC&G said defeatedly.

"Then how do you get to it?"

"Exactly how you think. You jackhammer up the slab."

The rest of the day is pretty much a blur. I don't have any desire to remember anything else about that day.

Act II

Well, all was not lost, because first we needed confirmation that the sewer pipe was indeed broken. For that, we just needed someone with a flexible camera that could be threaded down a pipe. I had no idea there was such a thing, but there is. Apparently, it's kind of like a colonoscopy, except no one offers you anesthesia and you have to be awake for the entire invasive procedure.

Not that we would know this first hand, mind you. As it turns out, there was precisely one plumbing company in town with such a camera, and they would not, for any amount of money, consent to come to our house to scope our sewer pipe because – are you ready? – if they stuck their camera *designed to view the inside of pipes* down our sewer pipe, it might break. No appeals to logic, or, indeed, offers to just buy them a whole new camera that they could throw away if it broke, would change their minds.

So, after approval by our insurance, we found a company that would handle the whole deal. With their help, we moved the entire back half of our house into the front living room. Every cabinet, every picture on the wall, every piece of furniture, all of it moved into the living room or up into the spare bedroom. Then, our workers sealed off the living room and various entrances with plastic and tape, and they prepared to jackhammer up our slab.

At the time, I was working part-time as an instructor at a local college, and I left that day thinking that this wasn't going to be too bad.

I returned from work and, hand to heart, it looked like someone had been re-enacting *The Grapes of Wrath* in my house. Dust clouds hung in the air, swirling and obscuring your vision. And, once I made it through the dust and into the kitchen, there it was.

There was a three-foot deep, 15 foot long trench through my house, running from the kitchen, through the pantry, across the downstairs hallway, and into the guest bathroom.

To their credit, the workers had done an impressively neat job of the work, once you took into account that they were wielding a jackhammer in places a jackhammer was never intended to go. But, as it turned out, they started at the bathroom end and excavated the pipe toward the kitchen until they found the break: at the joint where the sewer pipe met the drain pipe from the sink.

Let me let you think about that for a minute. Had they started in the kitchen – or, had we had someone with a flexible camera willing to shove it two feet down our kitchen drain – we would have known that the break was essentially right within the slab under the kitchen counter. Sure, there would have been some destruction, and I probably would have freaked out anyway, but it would have been a problem that required relatively little in the way of jackhammering

A Pumpkin Pie Worth Leaving Tennessee For

and pouring of concrete. But now the damage had been done, and we had to live with the repair.

Act III

The problem with not having a sewer pipe hooked up in your kitchen, in addition to a gaping trench in there, is that you lose the use of your water, your disposal, and, until they haul it back in from its temporary spot in the dining room, your stove. This makes eating a little difficult because, while you can still microwave, cleaning up the dishes requires washing them in a dishpan and then taking the dirty water outside and throwing it in the yard. Since it was now December, this was no one's favorite job. We spent part of the subsequent May rescuing flatware from the yard before we started mowing that year.

Our workers proceeded with, well, absolutely no speed at all. Part of this was because it was now Christmas. I had to call them and ask nicely if they would hook up my stove so that I could make us something more than reservations over the holiday.

Part of it was because my tile shop was mad at me. I wanted to replace the vinyl, Formica, and nasty carpet that were originally in the kitchen, on the island countertop, and in the hallway, but I wouldn't opt for any of the expensive choices and complex layouts that would make this a good before-and-after story for their design portfolios. So, since I didn't want granite and mosaic tiles laid on the diagonal, they were going to make me wait.

In the meantime, Mr. FC&G started having to go out of town for work, and I was left home to manage this. I was only going to be out of class for a couple more weeks of Christmas break, and I pushed to get the big parts of the job done while I was home, but of course the project dragged into the beginning of the semester.

"Oh, ma'am, we're bonded! Just leave the house unlocked and we'll let ourselves in!"

Like hell. Pardon my French.

So, I spent the next two months giving the workers set hours that they could be in the house and shooing them out when I had to leave. This made for some interesting schedules. For one thing, it necessarily made me the first stop on their route each day, so I was getting up at about 5:30 to let workers in the house so they could do a little bit of work and leave by lunch time.

I tried to disguise the fact that I was home alone without my husband, but I was running out of places he could possibly be at 6:00 every morning. At a certain point, I resigned myself to the fact that my life had turned into a situation in which every day I waited for a panel van to show up in my driveway, and I would let two or three strangers into my house to do heaven knows what while I tried to write. One day, I went downstairs to get something and found my tile guy rummaging through my cabinets looking for a coffee mug. When he grabbed one of my good ones (mostly I only have printed coffee mugs that people give me as speaker gifts; no one ever thinks to give the guest speaker a bag of coffee beans), I offered to make a pot of coffee.

"No need," he said. It turned out that he just wanted to use my good mug to measure the water so that he could mix a batch of mortar. I just sighed and went back upstairs.

Act IV

As I mentioned, Mr. FC&G was doing some travelling for business and was on a per diem (read: paid restaurant meals), but I was home alone. And, since my kitchen facilities were limited for most of this endeavor, I had pretty much stopped eating. There were a good three months that I subsisted on granola bars, cashews, and cookies – anything that wouldn't require me to do dishes and throw flatware into the yard.

So, when May arrived, the project was nearly done, and I was literally on my last nerve. I was having panic attacks and was basically shaking all the time. And that was when a man I'll call BK came to town.

A Pumpkin Pie Worth Leaving Tennessee For

BK is the world's best ballroom dancer, or at least he was. A professional ballroom dancer, BK has won championships in every ballroom discipline available when he was competing. BK doesn't walk across the floor; he floats while the angels sing and small birds come and light on his shoulders. And he is an absolutely ruthless ballroom coach, but he is not one that you dare miss if you have the slightest opportunity to take a lesson from him

When our project was nearly complete, BK was in town, and we booked lessons knowing full well we didn't have the time or the mental stability for the usual dressing-down one gets from him. But go to our lessons we did.

BK, who had relentlessly critiqued us and our sub-par cha-cha the previous visit to town, apparently figured out that we were not at our best, and he asked us what was up. We told him a highly abbreviated version of this story, ending with, "and that's why, once we finish up here tonight, we still have to go to Lowe's and pick out a kitchen sink."

He leveled his gaze at us and said, "stainless?"

I agreed and said that I had my eye on one of those three-basin sinks with the vegetable sink in the middle, but BK said no.

"Nope. What you want is a single basin sink. The whole thing, one basin. You won't ever use the others, but if you get a single large basin, you can defrost a turkey or wash your puppy."

We left the dance studio that night and drove to Lowe's and said, "BK wants us to get a single basin stainless steel kitchen sink" and handed the guy the measurements. And that's what we got.

I've never yet defrosted a turkey in that thing, and we wash the dog in the bathtub. I don't care. At least I know the world's best ballroom dancer picked my kitchen sink.

Jennifer Patterson Lorenzetti

The Annual Canning Meltdown

To say that I'm under a bit of stress recently would be an understatement.

Somehow, between July and October, I need to develop and deliver three conference presentations (one down, two to go), design a new course, and do the rest of my regularly scheduled work, including a side biz. I also need to keep up with the garden, since heaven knows I've been fussing and praying about this thing since February, depending on the savings in food expenditures giving us a little cushion through the summer and into the fall.

What this means, however, is that I am canning late at night, and my bravado at how good I am at doing that came to a crashing halt Saturday night with the first disaster and melt-down of the year.

It started when Mr. FC&G and I were taking turns in the kitchen. The dishwasher was running, dishes were piling up, and I'm trying to rinse vegetables and fill a canner.

Of course, the canner, which I had balanced on the side of the sink, tipped over, hitting the colander of veggies and dumping them into the sink. I rescued them, rinsed them off, got the canner going, cooked the veggies (extra, just in case of any bacteria from the sink), and filled the jar.

And then the jar wouldn't stand up in the canner. And then I couldn't pick it up with the jar lifter. And then I started to scream bloody murder. Mr. FC&G, who has been known to observe and participate in a few meltdowns in the factories he works in, calmly asked, "do you need help?"

If I didn't know that he doesn't relish witnessing me have a full scale, blood vessel popping meltdown, I'd still be cleaning pickles off the far wall. As it was, we got the rack out of the canner, reseated the jar, and processed those $#%& pickles.

A Pumpkin Pie Worth Leaving Tennessee For

They'd better taste like manna from heaven, that's all I have to say.

Jennifer Patterson Lorenzetti

Interlude: On a Day Working in the Fall Garden

I do not like your wretched fall.
I do not like the fall at all!
I do not like the falling leaves.
I do not like to wear long sleeves.

You may have your herbal tea.
Keep your soup far from me.
I do not want a cozy fire.
Sun and heat I desire.

I do not want to drive in snow.
I won't wear boots wherever I go.
I do not want to stay inside
Of this house where I reside.

I do not want to wear a sweater.
Shorts and flip flops would be better.
I want to garden all year round,
And live in a small beach town.

So keep your fall, if you please.
I'll winter in the Florida Keys!

ABOUT THE AUTHOR

Jennifer Patterson Lorenzetti had her first garden – and her first compost pile – at the age of eight. Since then, she's been passionate about gardening, traditional homemaking, and saving time and money.

As a professional writer, she is the owner of Hilltop Communications. She also teaches design history for Miami University and Wittenberg University, and she is a sought-after speaker on a variety of topics.

www.ingramcontent.com/pod-product-compliance
Lightning Source LLC
Chambersburg PA
CBHW071724040426
42446CB00011B/2209